GETTING AROUND

UNDER THE SEA

Lynn M. Stone

Rourke Publishing LLC
Vero Beach, Florida 32964

www.rourkepublishing.com

PHOTO CREDITS:
All photos © Lynn M. Stone except cover, pgs 7, 8, 12 © Marty Snyderman

EDITORIAL SERVICES:
Pamela Schroeder

Library of Congress Cataloging-in-Publication Data

Stone, Lynn M.
    Getting around / Lynn M. Stone
      p. cm. — (Under the sea)
    Includes bibliographical references (p.).
    ISBN 1-58952-110-2
     1. Marine animals—Locomotion—Juvenile literature.
    [1. Marine animals—Locomotion.] I. Title.

QL122.2 .S79 2001
591.77—dc21   2001019424

Printed in the USA

TABLE OF CONTENTS

OCEAN LOCOMOTION

Locomotion is the way that an animal moves. In the ocean, for example, many animals swim. That is their way of locomotion. You may have seen skillful ocean swimmers such as sharks, seals, and porpoises.

Not all **marine** animals are good swimmers. In fact, many of them, like starfish, sea urchins, and most snails, don't swim at all.

A tarpon's torpedo shape and sharply forked tail help it swim fast.

SWIMMERS

The biggest and fastest of marine animals are swimmers. But marine swimmers have different shapes and even different body parts. They don't all swim the same way.

Different **species** of fish may swim fast or slowly. If they're fast, they have slim, rocket-shaped bodies, thin fins, and forked tails. If they're slow, they often have short, plump, or flat bodies.

Marbled ribbontail rays swim with flaps of their broad "wings".

Most fish **propel** themselves forward by movements of muscles along their sides. Fins help a fish rise and sink in the water. They work like brakes and steering wheels, too.

Most kinds of fish have an **air bladder**. The air bladder is like a balloon inside a fish. The amount of air in it helps a fish swim up toward the surface or down to the sea bottom. More air in the bladder helps the fish float upward. Less air helps the fish swim deep. Sharks and their cousins, the rays, don't have air bladders. Their fins and tails do some of the work air bladders do in other fish.

The long, sharp fins and snout of an oceanic white-tip shark help it glide through the sea.

Ocean swimmers like seals and sea turtles don't have fins. They do have paddle-like legs called flippers. Flippers are as useful to seals and turtles as fins are to fish. A penguin has no fins or flippers. It does have flat, narrow wings. Underwater, a penguin uses its wings to swim. A penguin's wings are too small for real flight, but penguins fly underwater!

Whales have wide, flat tails called **flukes**. A whale swims by pumping its flukes up and down.

A whale's flukes give it undersea swimming power.

The olive sea snake has a paddle-shaped tail to help it swim.

A marine turtle's long, flat flippers propel it through the sea.

Sea otters love to float on their backs on the sea surface. Underwater, they swim with the movement of their long, strong tails and webbed hind feet.

Another marine **mammal**, the West Indian manatee, has a wide, flat tail to propel it. Some sea snakes have flat tails to help them swim, too.

A harbor seal's flippers power its backstroke.

Octopus and squid have no fins, flippers, wings, or tails. But they can swim very fast. What's their secret? An octopus can fill its body with water. By forcing the water out, the octopus zooms forward. The octopus is like a balloon filled with air. If the air rushes out all at once, the balloon flies forward.

The sea hare (see title page) is squishy and flat, a big snail without a shell. It swims by flexing its body back and forth, much like you would flex a muscle.

A red octopus swims across a sandy ocean bottom.

DRIFTERS

Marine drifters are like leaves in a river. Drifters go wherever the ocean currents take them. They have little or no control over where they go.

The Portuguese man-of-war is a common drifter along Florida's east coast. Marine drifters make up the "stew" of floating plants and animals called **plankton**. Most plankton animals are much smaller than the man-of-war. Many of them are too small to see.

One of the floaters, a Portuguese man-of-war is pushed ashore by wind and ocean currents.

CRAWLERS AND WALKERS

Some sea animals don't float or swim. They may crawl, walk, or dig. Lobsters and crabs are walkers. Their legs aren't very useful for swimming. But their legs are fine for walking along the sea bottom.

Sea urchins, starfish, and sea cucumbers crawl along on tiny "feet" that move by water power. A snail or clam crawls with a thick, soft "foot" that reaches out of the animal's shell. The foot can also dig into soft sea soil.

An ochre sea star crawls among purple sea urchins.

The scallop is an unusual clam. It swims short distances by clapping its two matching shell halves together.

The frogfish is unusual, too. Instead of swimming, it uses its fins as walking sticks!

GLOSSARY

air bladder (AYR BLAD er) — a balloon-like, air-filled organ that helps a fish rise, sink, and stay balanced in the water

flukes (FLOOKS) — the tail of a great whale

mammal (MAM el) — any one animal in the group of air-breathing, warm-blooded, milk-producing animals with hair or fur

marine (meh REEN) — of the sea

plankton (PLANGK ten) — the usually tiny, floating plants and animals of the seas

propel (preh PEL) — to power something's movement; to push

species (SPEE sheez) — within a group of closely related animals, such as whales, one certain kind (*humpback* whale)

INDEX

Further Reading

Bailey, Jill. *How Fish Swim*. Marshall Cavendish, 1996

Kalman, Bobbie and Walker, Niki. *How Do Animals Move?* Crabtree, 2000

Marquitty, Miranda. *Ocean*. Dorling Kindersley, 1995

Seward, H. *Rays*. Rourke Publishing, 1998

Websites To Visit

http://www.top20biology.com

About The Author

Lynn Stone is the author of over 400 children's books. He is a talented natural history photographer as well. Lynn, a former teacher, travels worldwide to photograph wildlife in their natural habitat.